J 546.513
Watt
Watt, Susan

Zirconium

THE ELEMENTS

Zirconium

Susan Watt

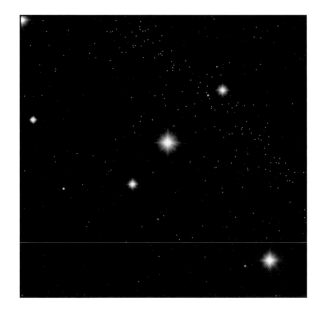

 **Marshall Cavendish**
Benchmark

New York

Marshall Cavendish Benchmark
99 White Plains Road
Tarrytown, New York 10591

www.marshallcavendish.us

Library of Congress Cataloging-in-Publication Data

Watt, Susan, date
Zirconium / Susan Watt.
p. cm. — (The elements)
Includes index.
ISBN 978-0-7614-2688-2
1. Zirconium--Juvenile literature. 2. Chemical elements--Juvenile
literature. I. Title.

QD181.Z7W38 2008
546'.513--dc22

2007060885

1 6 5 4 3 2

Printed in Malaysia

Picture credits
Front Cover: Alamy: Dinodia Images
Back Cover: Shutterstock

Alamy: Dinodia Images 14
Stan Celestain: 10b
Corbis: Document General Motors/Reuter R. 30, M. A. Pushpa Kumara 13, Roger Ressmeyer 7, 18b, 19, Jim Sugar 12, 27
Getty Images: 9, AFP 3, 15, Time & Life Pictures 6
Shutterstock: Vadim Kozlovsky 22, Gordon Swanson 20
Science & Society Picture Library: Science Museum 17
Science Photo Library: 16, Dee Breger 11, Klaus Guldbrandsen 24, Roger Harris 1, 10t,
Russ Lappa 4, 18t, Maximilian Stock Ltd 25, Peter Menzel 26
University of Pennsylvania Library: Edgar Fahs Smith Collection 8bl, 8br.

Series created by The Brown Reference Group plc.
Designed by Sarah Williams
www.brownreference.com

Contents

What is zirconium?

Zirconium is a metal—but not one that you are likely to come across among the metal objects you use at home. Despite this, zirconium is a common element. There is a lot of it in the rocks that make up Earth's surface. However, zirconium is difficult to purify, and until recently, it had few uses.

Gemstones and other uses

The most common use of zirconium might be a surprise. The metal is used to make gemstones—the sparkling crystals in jewelry. People have known about the natural gemstone zircon for thousands of years. We now know that zircon is a compound of zirconium. (A compound is a substance that is formed when two or more elements react.) However, pure zirconium was only extracted from its compounds about two hundred years ago. Today, imitation diamonds are made from cubic zirconia. These jewels are an artificial gemstone made from a zirconium compound. Zirconium has many other uses, including making medicines and in the components of nuclear reactors.

Inside zirconium atoms

Zirconium is the fortieth element listed in the periodic table and has the chemical symbol Zr. Like all elements, zirconium is made up of atoms. These tiny particles contain even smaller particles called protons, neutrons, and electrons.

Protons and neutrons have about the same mass and are found in the nucleus (center) of the atom. Electrons are much lighter and move around the nucleus.

All zirconium atoms have 40 protons in the nucleus. That number is known as the element's atomic number. The number of electrons in an atom is always the same as the number of protons. However, the number of neutrons in each atom varies. Some zirconium atoms have as many as 56 neutrons in the nucleus, while others have just 50. The number of protons and neutrons in an atom's nucleus is called its atomic mass number.

Pure zirconium is a soft and shiny metal. The metal reacts with oxygen and nitrogen in the air. That forms a dull gray layer on the surface.

Atoms of the same element with different atomic mass numbers are called isotopes. Zirconium has five different isotopes. The most common is Zr-90. This isotope has an atomic mass number of 90 (40 protons + 50 neutrons = 90). About half of all zirconium atoms are Zr-90. The least common isotope of zirconium is Zr-96. This isotope is radioactive. Its nucleus is unstable and breaks apart, releasing particles and radiation.

Electron layers

The 40 electrons in zirconium atoms are arranged in layers, or shells, around the nucleus. Each shell can hold a certain number of electrons. The electrons in the outermost shell determines how the atom reacts. A zirconium atom has two electrons in its outermost shell.

ZIRCONIUM

Nucleus

First shell

Second shell

Third shell

Fourth shell

Fifth shell

Each atom of zirconium contains 40 electrons orbiting a tiny central nucleus of protons and neutrons. The electrons are in 5 shells around the nucleus. The first shell has 2 electrons, the second shell has 8, and the third shell has 18. The outer 2 shells are incomplete. The fourth shell has 10 of its 18 spaces filled, while the fifth, and outermost, shell has 2 of 8 spaces occupied.

DID YOU KNOW?

ZIRCONIUM ISOTOPES

Isotope	No. of neutrons	Proportion in nature
Zr-90	50	51.5 percent
Zr-91	51	11 percent
Zr-92	52	17 percent
Zr-94	54	17.5 percent
Zr-96	56	3 percent

Special characteristics

Zirconium is unremarkable to look at. Like other more familiar metals, it is a shiny, gray-white solid. Its density is much like the density of iron. (Density is a measure of how heavy a substance is compared to its volume.) Sometimes zirconium is ground into a powder. This powder is blue-black instead of gray.

Chemical properties

Corrosion is the process that weakens metals as they react with air, water, and other compounds. Zirconium is very resistant to corrosion. It is used to make alloys—mixtures of metals—that do not corrode. Zirconium alloys are used to make tanks, pipes, and pumps for factories that make reactive chemicals. These chemicals would corrode and damage components made from alloys that did not contain zirconium.

Completely pure zirconium is soft and can be shaped easily. However, zirconium containing even a tiny amount of other elements becomes very hard and shatters easily when hammered.

Most metals are poisonous to the human body, but zirconium is not. As a result, objects made from zirconium can be used inside the body without affecting a person's health.

Zirconium is not completely safe, though. It can explode and be a serious fire hazard. When pure zirconium is ground into a fine powder it can catch fire suddenly, so safety precautions are needed when working with the metal.

ZIRCONIUM FACTS	
● Atomic number	40
● Atomic mass number	91 (average)
● Melting point	3371 °F (1855 °C)
● Boiling point	7900 °F (4371 °C)
● Density	6.5 grams per cubic cm (6.5 times the density of water).

DID YOU KNOW?

Zirconium compounds can be used to make large flames. These flame-producing qualities have been employed to make some terrifying weapons. Dragon's Breath is a zirconium-containing powder used in a shotgun. When the gun is fired, flames erupt from the barrel like a flamethrower. Soldiers and police sometimes use Dragon's Breath weapons during riots to frighten away crowds. The substance is banned in most countries because it is very dangerous.

Other properties

Zirconium has a high melting point and stays hard even when it is very hot. That makes it useful for making things that must stay strong at high temperatures. The metal can conduct heat and electricity, but not as well as most metals. Pure zirconium is also ductile. That means that it is easy to make it into thin wires or sheets.

Neutrons are released by radioactive atoms, such as those in nuclear fuel. Most metals block streams of neutrons. However, zirconium lets these particles pass straight through. As a result zirconium is used to make tubes for holding this fuel inside a nuclear reactor. The tubes do not melt at the high temperatures inside the reactor and allow neutrons to pass through.

A technician prepares a zirconium container before pouring melted nuclear fuel into it.

Zirconium in history

Zirconium is named for the mineral zircon, which has been used as a jewel for centuries. Zircons are mentioned in the Bible. They were one of the twelve gems worn by the high priests of Israel.

Zircon comes in many colors and sometimes as colorless stones that have a brilliant sparkle when they are cut. For this reason, the stones were thought for a long time to be a soft type of diamond.

Jöns Jakob Berzelius was the first person to purify zirconium.

Martin Klaproth discovered zirconium in 1789.

A scientist welds zirconium inside an airless chamber during the 1950s. Welding the metal in air would make it catch fire.

Investigating zircon

In 1789 the German chemist Martin Klaproth showed that zircons were not diamonds at all. He heated zircon with a reactive compound called sodium hydroxide. The two substances reacted to make an oxide, a compound containing oxygen atoms. Klaproth realized that the oxide contained a new element. He called the oxide zirconia, and the element was named zirconium.

Klaproth was unable to produce pure zirconium. It was 35 years later, in 1824, that the Swedish chemist Jöns Jakob Berzelius first made a sample of pure zirconium metal. Several other chemists had been trying to to do this. Berzelius succeeded by heating a mixture of potassium and potassium zirconium fluoride in an iron tube. He obtained a black powder that was 93 percent zirconium, but he could not purify it further. It was not until almost one hundred years later that high-purity zirconium could be made. This delayed progress in studying the element.

DID YOU KNOW?

The name *zirconium* comes from *zircon*, the name of the element's main mineral. *Zircon* comes from the Persian word *zargun*, meaning "gold color." It is thought to refer to the color of some zircon gemstones. Zircons actually come in a wide variety of colors, including red, brown, green, and yellow, or they can be colorless.

Zirconium in nature

Zirconium is found across the universe. Most of the stars that glow with a red light contain titanium. However, some red stars have zirconium.

Although many people have not heard of it, zirconium is not a rare element in nature. Zirconium is more common in Earth's crust than many more familiar metals, such as lead, copper, zinc, mercury, nickel, and tin. In fact, there is about as much zirconium on Earth as there is carbon—the element that forms the basis of all life on Earth. Moon rocks have even more zirconium than Earth's rocks. The Sun contains only a very tiny amount of

zirconium. But some cooler stars, which glow with a red light, contain a larger amount of the element.

Compounds

Zirconium is never found in nature as a pure metal. That is because it is a reactive element and bonds with other elements to form compounds.

Natural compounds are known as minerals. Zircon is the most common zirconium mineral. Its scientific name is zirconium silicate ($ZrSiO_4$). Another zirconium mineral is baddelyite, which contains zirconium oxide (ZrO_2).

Zircon is a hard mineral that contains zirconium, silicon, and oxygen atoms.

DID YOU KNOW?

PROPORTIONS IN NATURE

Source	Amount per kilogram
Earth's crust	165 milligrams
Moon rock	370 milligrams
Meteorites	7 milligrams
Sun	0.4 milligrams
Universe	0.5 milligrams
Human body	0.5 milligrams

Mining minerals

Rocks containing zircon and baddelyite are found across the world. Each year, around 1,375,000 tons (1,250,000 tonnes) of zirconium minerals are mined. The main countries that produce zirconium minerals are Australia, South Africa, and Ukraine. Some other countries, including China, India, Brazil, and the United States, also produce smaller amounts.

Rock types

Zirconium minerals are found in all types of rock. They are most common in sandy areas, such as beaches and riverbeds. For example, pebbles of baddeleyite from the coast of Brazil contain more than 90 percent zirconium oxide.

The oldest rock in the world, which has been magnified 5,000 times, is nearly 4 billion years old and contains tiny zircon crystals.

Ancient stones

Besides being a source of zirconium, the mineral zircon has some other interesting properties. Zircon crystals are very tough so they are not broken apart as easily as other minerals. Over millions and even billions of years, rocks are crushed, worn away, and heated deep underground. While the minerals around the zircon crystals crumble away and turn into clay and sand, the zircon crystals remain intact. As a result, the oldest objects on Earth are probably zircons. Some have survived through the planet's whole history.

Zirconium gems

The mineral zircon is also used as a gemstone, or jewel. Zircon is not very rare, so it is classified as a "semi-precious" gem. Because they are rare and are in high demand, only diamonds, rubies, sapphires, and emeralds are called "precious" stones.

Zircons occur in a wide range of natural colors. They can look very beautiful because their crystals sparkle like a diamond when cut correctly.

Colored jewels

Zircons have been used as gemstones throughout history. They occur in different parts of the world. For this reason, the gem

A chemist studies zircons found in Australia. The centers of some of these crystals were formed 4.4 billion years ago, making them the world's oldest crystals ever dated in a laboratory.

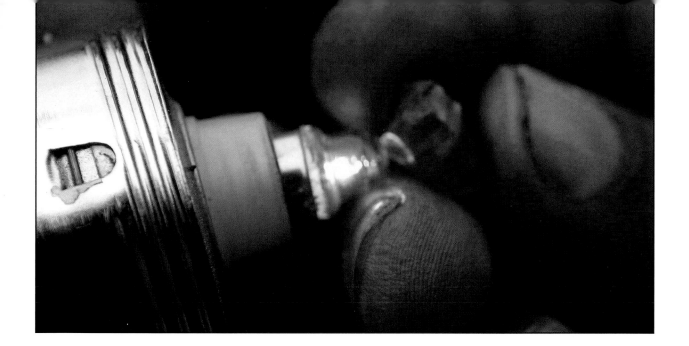

A jewel merchant inspects the quality of a zircon from Sri Lanka by shining a light into the crystal.

has acquired a variety of different names. The name *jargon* (or *jargoon*) also means "zircon," and comes from the same Arabic word—*zargun*. Today, the name jargon is generally used for pale or smoke-colored zircon stones.

Another name for zircon gems is hyacinth, or sometimes jacinth. These names now refer to the yellow, orange, or reddish zircons, which are the most common colors.

Colorless zircon stones are sometimes called Matara diamonds, after the Matara region of Sri Lanka, which is a famous source of these stones. Until zirconium was discovered in zircons, stones from Matara were thought to be just low-quality diamonds. Pure zircon crystals are colorless, but they are rare in nature.

Adding color

The color of zircons (or any other crystals) depends on what light they absorb. Colorless zircons absorb no light, so all the light passes through unchanged. You can look right through a colorless zircon, and everything looks the same color. A yellow zircon absorbs some types of

light, and only lets yellow light pass through it. As a result, the zircon looks yellow.

The many colors of zircons, which include green, pink, and even purple, come from impurities. These impurities include tiny amounts of iron or chromium, which are locked inside the zircon crystals. The impurities change the way the zircon crystals absorb light.

Colored zircons can be made colorless by heating them. The heat drives the impurities away, producing a clear crystal.

Zircons look best when they have been cut into certain shapes. The shapes make the light sparkle as it passes through the crystals.

Heat treatment is also used to produce striking blue zircons. Although the color is usually added to the stones in factories, blue zircons are among the most popular.

The color of a zircon can also be caused by changes in the way atoms are arranged inside the crystal. For example, the crystal structure is altered when a zircon is crushed and heated while buried deep underground.

Losing their sparkle

Diamonds are the hardest minerals on Earth and hardly wear away at all. Zircon gemstones are not as hard as diamonds, but they are hard enough to be cut into similar complex shapes. As zircon jewels become worn, chipped, and scratched, they gradually become less shiny and sparkle less.

DID YOU KNOW?

RADIOACTIVE JEWELS

Zircon gemstones can be very slightly radioactive. This is because they can contain a small amount of uranium or thorium atoms. These elements are naturally radioactive. Their atoms release radiation. A large amount of radiation is dangerous. However, zircons produce only tiny amounts of radiation and they are completely safe.

This necklace was made in 1928 for an Indian prince. The original necklace contained diamonds that disappeared when the necklace was lost for many years. The necklace was rediscovered in 1998 and its diamonds are now replaced by 2,930 cubic zirconia.

a substance. Zircons bend light more than most gems. They also bend some colors of light more than others. That is why zircons produce rainbow-colored sparkles.

Artificial gem

Since the 1970s, most gemstones have been made in factories. These jewels are made from a form of zirconium oxide known as cubic zirconia. A cubic zirconia gem looks just like a diamond but is less expensive. The only obvious difference is that cubic zirconia are much heavier than diamonds. Cubic zirconia is made by mixing calcium and yttrium compounds into melted zirconium oxide. The mixture is then cooled carefully so it forms cubic crystals.

Bending light

Shiny objects reflect light in the same way as a mirror. See-through objects, like a gemstone, also refract, or bend, light. This is what makes them appear to sparkle. All zircons have a very high refractive index. A refractive index is a measure of how much light bends as it passes through

DID YOU KNOW?

ZIRCONS IN MYTHOLOGY

In mythology, zircon jewels were once thought to protect the people who wore them. For example, zircons were said to protect travelers from dangers such as lightning, robbery, and deadly diseases. Zircons were also thought to help people to sleep. However, if the jewel lost its shine, then its owner would have bad luck.

Extracting and refining zirconium

Many thousands of tons of zirconium and zirconium compounds are produced each year. They come from zircon (zirconium silicate) and baddeleyite (zirconium oxide) minerals extracted from the ground.

Side by side

Wherever zirconium is found, it always occurs together with another element called hafnium. This metal is so similar to zirconium that it is very difficult to separate the two elements. Purified zirconium metal usually contains between 1 and 3 percent hafnium. For most uses of zirconium, the hafnium in it does not matter, since the two elements are so similar. However, solid hafnium absorbs neutrons, while zirconium lets them pass straight through. The zirconium tubes used to hold nuclear fuel have had the hafnium removed, so neutrons can escape from the tube. Hafnium is used in other parts of a nuclear reactor to collect neutrons.

Purifying zirconium

Until recently, the main method of extracting zirconium from its minerals was the Kroll process, which is also used for extracting the metal titanium. In this

William Kroll was an American chemist who developed the first process for purifying zirconium in large amounts.

process, the zirconium minerals are first converted to zirconium tetrachloride ($ZrCl_4$) gas. Any remaining minerals or contaminating compounds are removed from the gas. Any impurities that get into zirconium metal make it weak and shatter easily. The zirconium tetrachloride vapor is then reacted with magnesium metal, forming magnesium chloride ($MgCl_2$) and zirconium metal. All air and water vapor (steam) have to be kept away while this reaction takes place so they do not become involved. The magnesium chloride and any leftover magnesium are then removed. That produces granules of zirconium, which can be pressed into solid bars of pure zirconium metal.

Modern changes

The Kroll process is being replaced by a new way of processing zirconium. Most zirconium used today is in in the form of compounds, so less pure metal needs to be produced. Chlorine and chloride compounds are very harmful, so chemists try to avoid using them.

The metal blades of these scissors are coated with zirconium. The layer of zirconium stops the blades from rusting and becoming blunt.

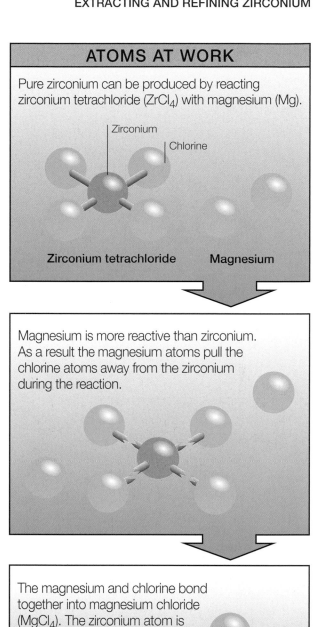

ATOMS AT WORK

Pure zirconium can be produced by reacting zirconium tetrachloride ($ZrCl_4$) with magnesium (Mg).

Zirconium

Chlorine

Zirconium tetrachloride   Magnesium

Magnesium is more reactive than zirconium. As a result the magnesium atoms pull the chlorine atoms away from the zirconium during the reaction.

The magnesium and chlorine bond together into magnesium chloride ($MgCl_4$). The zirconium atom is not bonded to anything and forms pure metal.

Zirconium   Magnesium chloride

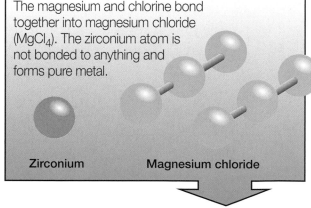

The reaction that takes place can be written like this:

$$ZrCl_4 + 2Mg \rightarrow 2MgCl_2 + Zr$$

DID YOU KNOW?

HAFNIUM, A CONSTANT COMPANION

Zirconium always occurs alongside another metal in nature. That metal is hafnium (Hf). Wherever zirconium is found in its two main minerals (zircon and baddelyite), there is always the same proportion of hafnium included. This is one atom of hafnium for every fifty atoms of zirconium. The elements exist together because they are very similar and natural processes affect them in the same way. Hafnium's atomic number is 72. Its atoms have 32 more protons and 32 more electrons than zirconium atoms. However, the atoms of the two elements are almost exactly the same size, so their properties are the same.

Pure hafnium looks very similar to pure zirconium.

The method used to purify zirconium today involves reacting zirconium silicate ($ZrSiO_4$) with sodium hydroxide (NaOH). That is done at very high temperatures (1100–1600 °F or 600-900 °C). The reaction makes sodium zirconate and sodium silicate. The silicate is washed away leaving sodium zirconate and small amounts of impurities. The impure sodium zirconate is purified further and at the same time converted into other useful zirconium compounds, plus some zirconium metal.

When zirconium for nuclear fuel rods is produced, the hafnium is removed by a process called ion exchange. The resulting hafnium-free zirconium costs considerably more to produce than the normal hafnium-contaminated metal.

Technicians pour nuclear fuel into a tube of pure zirconium that has had all the hafnium removed.

Zirconium compounds

Zirconium is a reactive metal. It forms compounds in the same way as most other metals. Metals generally form compounds with nonmetals. Nonmetals are elements that tend to have the opposite properties of metals. Metals are usually hard and shiny solids. Nonmetals are gases, such as oxygen and chlorine, or soft crumbly solids, such as sulfur or phosphorus.

Ionic compounds

When zirconium reacts with a nonmetal, the two elements form an ionic compound. Ionic compounds are made when atoms lose or gain electrons.

Atoms do not have an overall charge. That is because the negative charge of their electrons is balanced by the positive charge of their protons.

A piece of Moon rock brought to Earth by the Apollo *17 mission in 1972. Zirconium compounds are more common in Moon rock than in Earth's rocks.*

Atoms that lose or gain electrons become ions. Atoms that lose electrons have more protons than electrons. They become positively-charged ions. Atoms that gain electrons become negatively-charged ions.

Metals, including zirconium, lose electrons and form positively-charged ions. Nonmetals gain electrons and form ions with a negative charge. Opposites attract, so the positively-charged zirconium ions are drawn to negatively-charged nonmetal ions. The attraction bonds the ions together forming an ionic compound.

Zirconium ions

Most zirconium ions have a charge of +4. Chemists write this ion as Zr^{4+}. This ion forms when a zirconium atom loses two electrons from its outer electron shell and two more from the next shell in. Zr^{4+} ions form a bond with one or more ions with a total charge of −4. For example, in zirconium tetrafluoride (ZrF_4), a Zr^{4+} is bonded to four fluoride ions. These ions each have a charge of −1 and are written as F^-. Zirconium oxide (ZrO_2) also contains a Zr^{4+} ion. This time it is bonded to two oxide ions (O^{2-}).

A large drill is used to make a hole in concrete. The drill's bit (metal cutter) is coated with zirconium carbide, a very tough compound that prevents the bit from wearing away and becoming blunt.

However, some zirconium compounds are made with ions with charges of +2 or +3. For example, zirconium forms three different compounds with chlorine. $ZrCl_4$ contains a Zr^{4+} ion, but $ZrCl_3$ contains a Zr^{3+} ion, and $ZrCl_2$ contains a Zr^{2+} ion.

Covalent compounds

Zirconium also forms compounds by sharing electrons with other atoms. Instead of moving from one atom to another, an electron sits in the electron shells of two atoms at the same time. The electron belongs to both atoms and that bonds the atoms together. Compounds that have bonds like this are called covalent. Zirconium is an unusual metal because most metals do not form covalent bonds.

Complex compounds

Zirconium also forms complexes, which are held together with covalent bonds. A complex is made up of several different groups of atoms that are bonded to a central zirconium atom. The groups surrounding the zirconium atom provide all the electrons for the covalent bonds. These electrons sit in empty spaces in the zirconium atom's second outermost shell.

Zirconium bonds with three oxide ions to form a negatively-charged complex ion called a zirconate (ZrO_3^{2-}). This ion bonds with reactive metals, such as calcium or sodium.

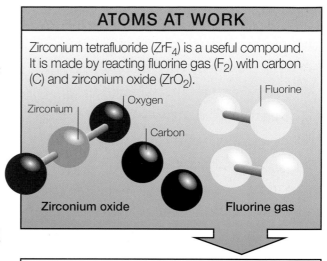

ATOMS AT WORK

Zirconium tetrafluoride (ZrF_4) is a useful compound. It is made by reacting fluorine gas (F_2) with carbon (C) and zirconium oxide (ZrO_2).

Zirconium   Oxygen   Fluorine
Carbon

Zirconium oxide   **Fluorine gas**

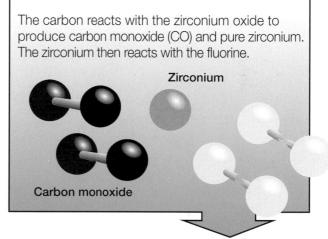

The carbon reacts with the zirconium oxide to produce carbon monoxide (CO) and pure zirconium. The zirconium then reacts with the fluorine.

Zirconium

Carbon monoxide

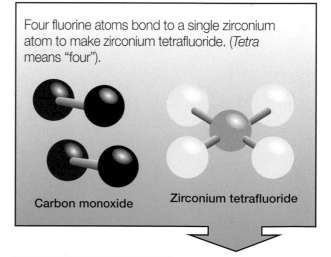

Four fluorine atoms bond to a single zirconium atom to make zirconium tetrafluoride. (*Tetra* means "four").

Carbon monoxide   **Zirconium tetrafluoride**

The reaction that takes place can be written like this:

$ZrO_2 + 2C + 2F_2 \rightarrow ZrF_4 + 2CO$

How zirconium reacts

Chemists think that zirconium and hafnium are more similar than any other pair of elements. What we know about zirconium chemistry is really about zirconium mixed with a little hafnium. But this does not matter much because the two elements always react in the same way.

Protective layer

Pure zirconium appears to be unreactive in air. It is because it is covered with a thin layer of zirconium oxide (ZrO_2) that forms when the metal reacts with the oxygen gas (O_2) in the air. If the layer of oxide is scratched away, the pure metal underneath is exposed. The metal begins to react again with the oxygen and another oxide layer will form within minutes.

The oxide layer also prevents zirconium from reacting with other compounds. For example, it does not react with most acids. An acid is a compound that contains a lot of hydrogen ions (H^+). A typical acid is hydrochloric acid (HCl). Zirconium does not react with alkalis either. Alkalis, such

Surgical tools are made from steel containing zirconium. The zirconium helps to prevent the steel from rusting and becoming dirty.

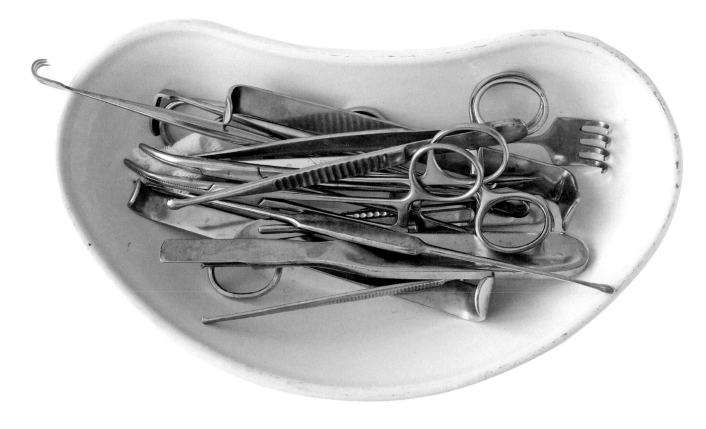

as sodium hydroxide (NaOH), are the opposite of acids. They are compounds that contain a lot of hydroxide ions (OH⁻).

However, zirconium does react with hydrofluoric acid (HF), one of the most reactive compounds known. The metal becomes more reactive when it is heated. The heat breaks the oxide layer apart, so the zirconium underneath can react.

Absorbing gas

Zirconium metal can absorb gases. The gas does not form a compound with the metal but sits in spaces between the zirconium atoms. Only gases containing small atoms, such as oxygen, nitrogen, and hydrogen, are absorbed. For every 100 atoms of zirconium, an extra 20 to 30 oxygen or nitrogen atoms can be held in the solid metal.

DID YOU KNOW?

FIRE AND WATER

Zirconium dust can explode without warning when it comes into contact with the air. The powdered metal is stored under water to keep the air away. However, if zirconium dust gets just slightly damp it becomes even more explosive. Damp dust particles react with the air more easily and explode even more violently than when dry. And if the zirconium is already burning, water will increase the blaze, rather than put it out. Firefighters must use gas to douse the flames.

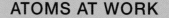

ATOMS AT WORK

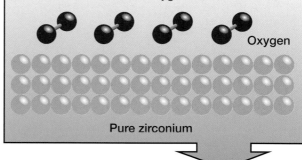

Zirconium reacts with oxygen (O_2) in the air to form zirconium oxide (ZrO_2). Zirconium atoms on the metal's surface meet oxygen atoms in the air.

Oxygen

Pure zirconium

Some of the zirconium atoms combine with the oxygen and form a layer of zirconium oxide on the surface.

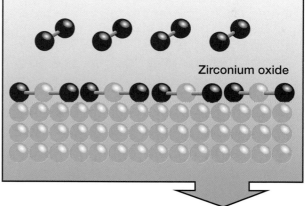

Zirconium oxide

The layer of oxide blocks more zirconium from reacting with oxygen. When the layer is scratched off, zirconium atoms are exposed to the air again. The scratched area is filled with zirconium oxide.

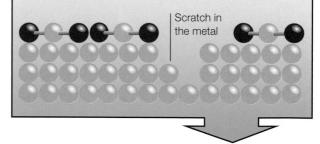

Scratch in the metal

The reaction that takes place can be written like this:

$$Zr + O_2 \rightarrow ZrO_2$$

Using zirconium

Zirconium oxide is the zirconium compound with the most uses. This compound is unaffected by high temperatures. Up to temperatures as high as 4800 °F (2700 °C), this compound neither burns nor melts. For this reason, zirconium oxide lines the furnaces used for melting metals. Very pure zirconium oxide is also used to make crucibles. These are containers are found in laboratories for heating substances to high temperatures.

Ceramics

Pure zirconium oxide is used to make super-strong ceramic materials. Zirconium oxide is mixed with yttrium oxide (Y_2O_3) and heated to a high temperature. The two compounds become mixed very thoroughly. One of them dissolves in the

A metal alloy is heated in an electric furnace. It heats substances using a stream of electric sparks that are as powerful as a bolt of lightning. The furnace is lined with zirconium oxide.

other, in the same way that sugar or salt mixes into warm water and disappears. When cooled, the material produced is very tough, as well as heat-resistant.

One use of zirconium ceramics is in replacement body parts, such as artificial hip and knee joints. A surgeon uses these to replace damaged joints so that injured people can stand and walk again. Zirconium ceramics are ideal for this job because they do not dissolve in water. If they did dissolve, the zirconium would slowly get into the blood and spread

---

DID YOU KNOW?

ZIRCONIUM KEEPS YOU FRESH

People who use a deodorant with antiperspirant may be putting a zirconium compound under their arms each morning. People sweat through tiny holes in the skin called pores. A compound named aluminum zirconium trichlorohydrex makes the cells surrounding the sweat pores expand so that the pores close. With the pores closed, no sweat can come out.

around the body. The ceramic body part would also gradually become weaker faster and break apart sooner.

This component from a car engine is made from a zirconium-containing ceramic. The component is stronger than one made from pure metal.

Cleaning exhaust

Another important use of zirconium oxide is in catalytic converters used by cars. The catalytic converters clean poisonous gases out of the exhaust produced by the car's engine. If these poisonous gases were released into the air, they would cause air pollution. The gases include carbon monoxide (CO) and nitric oxide (NO). They are converted into less dangerous gases by a catalyst, such as platinum. A catalyst makes a chemical reaction take place that would not occur on its own. However, the catalyst itself is unchanged by the reaction.

The gases coming from the car engine are hot, so zirconium oxide is used to make the catalytic converter heat-resistant. The zirconium compound also absorbs gases, so it acts as a supply of oxygen gas for the reactions happening inside the converter.

Zirconium metal

Until recently, the main use for zirconium metal was in nuclear fuel rods and parts of nuclear reactors. A single nuclear reactor could use half a million feet (150,000 meters) of zirconium alloy tubes. The zirconium tubes are used to hold the uranium fuel, making a fuel rod. The fuel rods are lowered into the center, or core, of the reactor, where they release heat. The reactor's core gets extremely hot, but the zirconium rods stay hard and strong even at these high temperatures.

The nuclear fuel releases neutrons. Neutrons are the particles that cause the chain reaction in a nuclear reactor. When neutrons emitted by one uranium atom hit another uranium atom, they make it break apart, producing heat and more neutrons. The heat produced is used to turn water into steam, which drives a generator to make electricity. The zirconium in the rods allows the neutrons to pass through and start the chain reaction. Other metals would block the neutrons.

Zirconium metal is also used to prevent other metals from corroding. For example, it is used in the latest bicycle frames. Zirconium's ability to soak up gases comes in handy in fluorescent lamps, such as neon lights. These tubes needs to be almost completely empty of gases to work. Zirconium is added to the tube to soak up any gases.

A researcher holds a disk made of layers of copper and zirconium. Each layer is just a few atoms thick, and the alloy is five times stronger than pure copper.

Zirconium dating

Geology is the science of how Earth's rocks form and change. Geologists study how minerals are squeezed and heated under the ground to make the rocks in Earth's crust. Zircon minerals are used to figure out the age of old rocks in a process is known as geological dating.

Zircons are very tough crystals and are unaffected by high temperatures and other geological processes. Because of this, the minerals stay the same for many millions of years after they have formed.

Radiation test

Geologists look for pieces of zircon in rocks. They can figure out how old these zircons are by measuring the amount of radioactive impurities in them. The impurities produce radiation, and older zircons produce less radiation than young ones. That is because the amount of radioactive impurities in the mineral gradually decreases as it gets older.

Important discoveries

Dating zircons has changed the way geologists think Earth formed. Early in Earth's development, the planet's surface was thought to be covered in hot liquid rocks. No liquid water could exist in these conditions. But researchers in Australia have found zircons that are 4.4 billion years old. That is just 200 million years younger than Earth itself. These zircons must have formed in cold rocks. This shows that at least some of the surface of the early Earth was solid rock and much cooler than had been thought before.

A scientist uses a microscope to study crystals of zircons to help figure out how old they are.

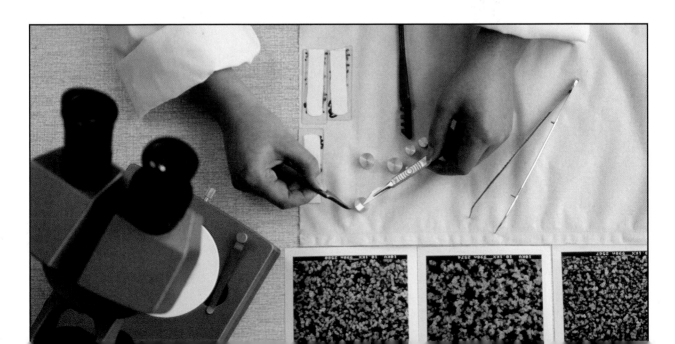

Periodic table

Everything in the universe is made from combinations of substances called elements. Elements are made of tiny atoms, which are the building blocks of matter.

The character of an atom depends on how many even tinier particles called protons there are in its center, or nucleus. An element's atomic number is the same as the number of its protons.

Scientists have found around 116 different elements. About 90 elements occur naturally on Earth. The rest have been made in experiments.

All these elements are set out on a chart called the periodic table. This lists all the elements in order according to their atomic number.

The elements at the left of the table are metals. Those at the right are nonmetals. Between the metals and the nonmetals are the metalloids, which sometimes act like metals and sometimes like nonmetals.

● On the left of the table are the alkali metals. These have just one outer electron.

● Metals get more reactive as you go down a group. The most reactive nonmetals are at the top of the table.

● On the right of the periodic table are the noble gases. These elements have full outer shells.

● The number of electrons orbiting the nucleus increases down each group.

● Elements in the same group have the same number of electrons in their outer shells.

● The transition metals are in the middle of the table, between Groups II and III.

Group I

Group II

Transition metals

1 H Hydrogen 1								
3 Li Lithium 7	4 Be Beryllium 9							
11 Na Sodium 23	12 Mg Magnesium 24							
19 K Potassium 39	20 Ca Calcium 40	21 Sc Scandium 45	22 Ti Titanium 48	23 V Vanadium 51	24 Cr Chromium 52	25 Mn Manganese 55	26 Fe Iron 56	27 Co Cobalt 59
37 Rb Rubidium 85	38 Sr Strontium 88	39 Y Yttrium 89	40 Zr Zirconium 91	41 Nb Niobium 93	42 Mo Molybdenum 96	43 Tc Technetium (98)	44 Ru Ruthenium 101	45 Rh Rhodium 103
55 Cs Cesium 133	56 Ba Barium 137	71 Lu Lutetium 175	72 Hf Hafnium 179	73 Ta Tantalum 181	74 W Tungsten 184	75 Re Rhenium 186	76 Os Osmium 190	77 Ir Iridium 192
87 Fr Francium 223	88 Ra Radium 226	103 Lr Lawrencium (260)	104 Rf Rutherfordium (263)	105 Db Dubnium (268)	106 Sg Seaborgium (266)	107 Bh Bohrium (272)	108 Hs Hassium (277)	109 Mt Meitnerium (276)

Lanthanide elements

Actinide elements

| 57
La
Lanthanum
39 | 58
Ce
Cerium
140 | 59
Pr
Praseodymium
141 | 60
Nd
Neodymium
144 | 61
Pm
Promethium
(145) |
| 83
Ac
Actinium
227 | 90
Th
Thorium
232 | 91
Pa
Protactinium
231 | 92
U
Uranium
238 | 93
Np
Neptunium
(237) |

The horizontal rows are called periods. As you go across a period, the atomic number increases by one from each element to the next. The vertical columns are called groups. Elements get heavier as you go down a group. All the elements in a group have the same number of electrons in their outer shells. This means they react in similar ways.

The transition metals fall between Groups II and III. Their electron shells fill up in an unusual way. The lanthanide elements and the actinide elements are set apart from the main table to make it easier to read. All the lanthanide elements and the actinide elements are quite rare.

Zirconium in the table

Zirconium is directly above hafnium in the table. Both elements are transition metals. Like other transition metals, zirconium atoms have empty spaces in their two outermost electron shells. Electrons in both these shells take part in chemical reactions. This allows zirconium atoms to form ions that have a variety of different charges.

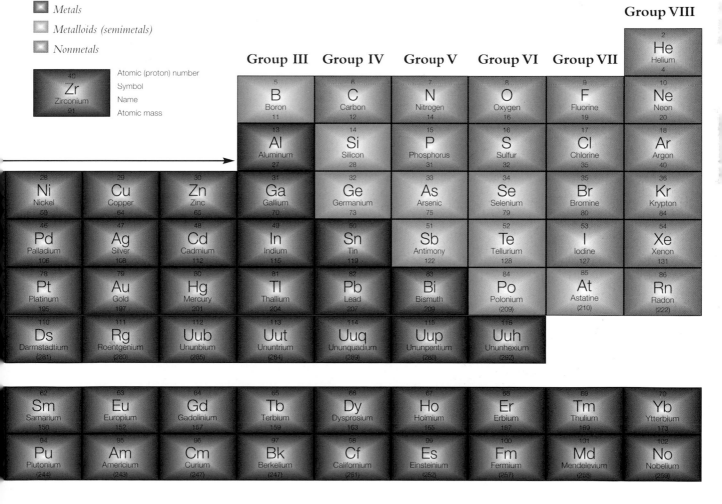

Chemical reactions

Chemical reactions are going on around us all the time. Some reactions involve just two substances, while others involve many more. But whenever a reaction takes place, at least one substance is changed.

In a chemical reaction, the atoms stay the same. But they join up in different combinations to form new molecules.

Writing an equation

Chemical reactions can be described by writing down the atoms and molecules before and after the reaction.

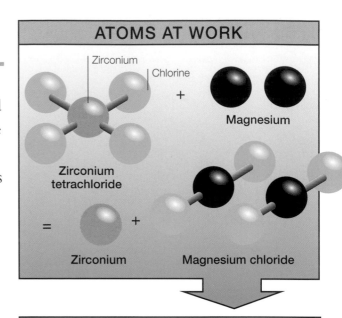

ATOMS AT WORK

Zirconium
Chlorine
+
Magnesium

Zirconium
tetrachloride

=   +

Zirconium   Magnesium chloride

The reaction that takes place when magnesium reacts with zirconium tetrachloride is written like this:

$$ZrCl_4 + 2Mg \rightarrow 2MgCl_2 + Zr$$

This tells us that a molecule of zirconium tetrachloride reacts with two atoms of magnesium to give two molecules of magnesium chloride and one atom of zirconium.

The honeycomb mesh inside a catalytic converter is coated with zirconium oxide.

Since the atoms stay the same, the number of atoms before the reaction will be the same as the number of atoms after the reaction. Chemists write the reaction as an equation. This shows what happens in the chemical reaction.

Making it balance

When the numbers of each atom on both sides of the equation are equal, the equation is balanced. If the numbers are not equal, something is wrong. So the chemist adjusts the number of atoms involved until the equation does balance.

Glossary

acid: An acid is a chemical that releases hydrogen ions easily during reactions.

alkali: A compound that releases hydroxide ions easily during reactions.

atom: The smallest part of an element that has all the properties of that element.

atomic mass number: The number of protons and neutrons in an atom.

atomic number: The number of protons in an atom's nucleus. Each element has a unique atomic number.

bond: The attraction between two atoms or ions that holds them together.

ceramic: A hard substance made of a mixture of a number of compounds.

compound: A substance made of two or more elements chemically joined together.

corrosion: The eating away of a material by reaction with oxygen and moisture.

crystal: A solid consisting of a repeating pattern of atoms, ions, or molecules.

dissolve: When a substance mixes with another very evenly so that one disappears.

electron: A tiny particle with a negative charge. Electrons move around the nucleus in layers called electron shells.

element: A substance that is made from only one type of atom.

ion: An atom or a group of atoms that has lost or gained electrons to become electrically charged.

isotopes: Atoms of an element with the same number of protons and electrons but different numbers of neutrons.

metal: An element on the left-hand side of the periodic table.

mineral: A compound or element as it is found in its natural form in Earth.

molecule: A unit that contains atoms held together by chemical bonds.

neutron: A tiny particle with no electrical charge. Neutrons are found in the nucleus of almost every atom.

nonmetal: An element on the right-hand side of the periodic table.

nucleus: The structure at the center of an atom containing protons and neutrons.

periodic table: A chart of all the chemical elements laid out in order of their atomic number.

proton: A tiny particle with a positive charge. Protons are found in the nucleus.

radiation: Particles and rays produced when a radioactive element decays.

radioactivity: A property of certain unstable atoms that causes them to release radiation.

reaction: A process in which two or more elements or compounds combine to produce new substances.

transition metal: An element positioned in the middle of the periodic table. As well as having spaces in their outer electron shell, most transition metals also have spaces in the next outermost shell.

Index